Operation – Clean-up day

Jason Tucker

Clink Street
London | New York

Published by Clink Street Publishing 2017

Copyright © 2017

illustrations by Nick Roberts

First edition.

The author asserts the moral right under the Copyright, Designs and Patents Act 1988 to be identified as the author of this work.

All rights reserved. No part of this publication may be reproduced, stored in a retrieval system or transmitted, in any form or by any means without the prior consent of the author, nor be otherwise circulated in any form of binding or cover other than that with which it is published and without a similar condition being imposed on the subsequent purchaser.

*ISBNs: 978-1-912262-32-8 paperback
978-1-912262-33-5 ebook*

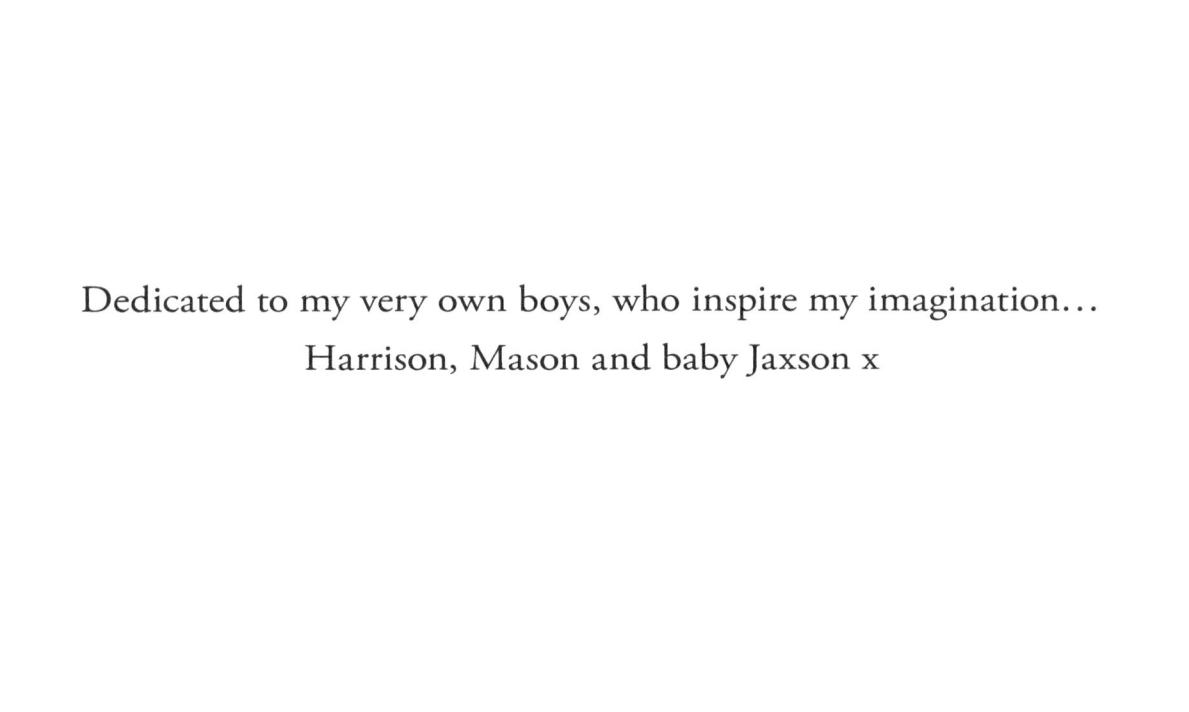

Dedicated to my very own boys, who inspire my imagination…
Harrison, Mason and baby Jaxson x

Jason Tucker

What a glorious day, hip hip hooray…
My brother and I are going to the swimming pool today…

But we can only go on one main condition…
We have to clear up all our toys, that is our mission!

Operation – Clean-up day

Mission 1 – The Lounge

Mummy says, the lounge is a good place to start this education…
But Mummy, we can't, that's our Grand Central Station…

Jason Tucker

We have over two million people passing through each day…
If we tidy away now, the trains will be in delay…
But Mummy said, if you want to get to the pool…
I'd pick it all up now, and stop being a fool.

Mission 2 – The Kitchen

Then to the kitchen, Mummy says, And in here too…
But Mummy, did you know this is the Castle of King Foo?

Jason Tucker

The knights are defending him from the evil ogre…
If we tidy away now, the King's reign will be over…
But Mummy said, come come – Just a few bits will do…
We need to get a move on, as it's almost a quarter to two!

Operation – Clean-up day

Mission 3 – The Hallway & Stairs

You need to tidy the hallway, I can't even walk up this staircase…
But Mummy, we can't, this is the ice mountain snow place.

Jason Tucker

The men have been climbing for weeks, they just can't stop…
If we tidy away now they won't get to the top…
But Mummy said, I suggest you clear this up and don't mess about…
You've still got upstairs to get on with, before we go out.

7

Operation – Clean-up day

Mission 4 – The Bedroom

Onto our bedroom, Mummy says, you have another place to sort…
But Mummy, we can't, this is our galactic space port…

Jason Tucker

The Thargoids and Zlatons are about to sign a peace truce…
If we tidy up now, all war could break loose…
But Mummy said, that's a chance I'm willing to take…
You can start with that spaceship that's near that toy snake.

Operation – Clean-up day

Mission 5 – The Bathroom

Mummy then says, getting into this
bathroom is a pain…
But Mummy, be careful – this is the
sea monsters' domain…

10

Jason Tucker

The pirates are circling, to catch him in sticky tape…
If we tidy away now, he's sure to escape…
But Mummy said, you've got two minutes to clean up this loo…
And please make sure you don't spill any more shampoo.

Operation – Clean-up day

Mission 6 – The Garden

Mummy says, clearing the toys in the garden is our final landmark…
But Mummy, do you know that's our dinosaur park?

Jason Tucker

If we take down the fences, the dinosaurs will get loose…
Our visitors will get eaten, and chewed until they're just juice.
But Mummy said, I think the visitors will be just fine…
Don't forget the T-Rex, who's tangled in that vine.

Operation - Clean-up day

Finally we're done, and off to the pool we go at last…
We could have gone earlier but we were just not that fast!
Next time we'll tidy up after each play time, I think…

Well mostly, well maybe, we'll see… wink wink…

Ingram Content Group UK Ltd.
Milton Keynes UK
UKHW020948190323
418726UK00005B/24